❦❦

Spiritual Perspectives

❦❦

Spiritual Perspectives

Gifts of a Prayerful Life

The Poetry of

Rev. Sharon E. Freeman

BASSWOOD PRESS

Copyright 2016 by Sharon E. Freeman

All rights reserved. No part of this publication may be reproduced or transmitted in any form or by any means, electronic or mechanical, including photocopy, recording, or any information storage and retrieval system, without permission in writing from the publisher except in the case of brief quotations embodied in critical articles and reviews.

Segments of the following poems are based on the specified Bible verses:

"Church"
It is not I but the Father within Who does the work. Jn. 14.10
Where two or three are gathered in my name, I am there among them. Mt. 18.20

"Shepherd"
Tend my sheep. Jn. 21.15-17

"Reverence for Life"
And God said, "It is Good." Gen. 1-2

"Powerlessness"
Blessed are the poor in spirit for theirs is the kingdom of Heaven. Mt. 5.3
The last will be first and the first will be last. Mt. 19.30

Cover photo: Sunset on the Sea of Galilee near Capernaum, www.christusrex.org.

Editing and book and cover design: Peggy Henrikson, Heart and Soul Editing

ISBN-10: 0692753818
ISBN-13: 978-0692753811

Printed in the United States of America
First Edition

BASSWOOD PRESS

Contents

Preface vii
My Ponderings and Learnings 1
   Hidden 2
   Uninvited 4
   Know Yourself 5
   Inside Out 6
   Helping Hands 8
   Share the Walk 10
   Hope 11
   Lifeline 12
   Loneliness 14
   Thief 16
   Demons 17
   Light of God 18
   It's Good 20
   Companions 21
   Church 22
   An Unseemly Cradle 23
   Shepherd 24
   Divine Discontent 25
   Feelings 26
   When Friends Leave 27
   Community 28
   Birdhouse in Your Soul 30
   Grace 31
   Reassurance 32
   Search for Myself 33
   Insecurity 34
   Good Enough 35
   Personality Trait 36
   Unfinished 38

Surrender to Time	39
Growing Pains	40
Weather Maker	41
How Do We Hear?	42
On Becoming Independent	44
Being Present	46
Will and Awareness	48
Peace	50
Diversity	51
Courage	52
Walking Around Blind	53
Striving	54
Reverence for Life	56
Imagine	58
Freedom	60
Presence	62
Evolution of Consciousness	63
Aging	64
Questions	65
Perfect Love	66
Powerlessness	67
God Cares	68
Family Night	69
Love Is a Choice	70
Living with Intention	71
Spiritual Guidance	72
Whose Energy Is It?	74
Jesus and Me	75
Walking Contemplation: A Word Picture	76
Requiescat	80
About the Author	81

Preface

Most of my adult life, I have kept a prayer journal. Frequently, I was moved to write a poem as a way of expressing my heartfelt response to a prayer session. I enjoyed writing these poems and often took them out to review them during my prayer time each day. They told me the story of Spirit's movement in my life. During times of stress, they became a solace as I read about the impact of prayer on my state of mind. They were a comfort to me and a reminder of God's real presence. They helped me see the opportunities for personal growth.

I have lived with rheumatoid arthritis for many years and have had frequent extended periods of intense pain. God was unmistakably present to me when I was suffering. I could manage these times when I had a Companion to walk through them with me. I found this was also true of other stressful times that are typical in everyday life. Loneliness, self-judgment, family dynamics, and the balance between career and home were some of the issues that sent me to prayer. Prayers of gratitude for my family and the life we shared in God's beautiful world were a daily practice.

Prayer is a way of life for me.

During the last year, I have been moved to share these writings with my family. Over time, others have seen them, too. Their support and my own intuition have led me to publish my poems with the intention of encouraging others.

My hope is they will inspire and help you in some way.

Rev. Sharon Freeman

My Ponderings and Learnings

Hidden

Under the paper
in my dresser drawer
lie the secret learnings
of a lifetime.

Not like the dust balls
under the bed,
these get brought out sometimes
for pondering,
    and reflection,
        and, sometimes,
sharing with someone
who would understand.

There,
in a brown envelope,
getting fatter with years
and smelling of sachet,
is the essence of me.
My thoughts and concerns,
    tears and joy,
        love and yearnings . . .
           growth.

Maybe someday
I'll take them out of the envelope
and put them in a book
for everyone to see.

That would be scary.
Then everyone would know me,
and I would have no safe secrets
   under the paper
      in my dresser drawer.

Uninvited

YOU come in the night,
stomping and pulling,
using my body
for a punching bag.

Whoever you are,
you leave me hurting,
aching,
limp as a rag.

It's not right
to come uninvited,
leaving life's needs so whole
and me so broken.

Who invited you anyway?
I don't remember
writing "Arthritis"
on any invitation.

Know Yourself

You are Spirit.
That is all you need
to know.

Beyond this body
that does your work
here on earth,
there is a spirit
that is you.

You are here to learn.

Spirit is triumphant
over matter.
Spirit does not die.
So bring that light
into the world.

Teach only love.

Bring spirit
into everything you do.
Live out of spirit.
It is your highest self
and your connection
to God.

Know yourself;
do your work.
Your work is
Love in action.

Inside Out

People ask,
"How are you today?"
I've forgotten how to say
"Fine."
That's what most people
want to hear.

If we could talk about
my inside,
I could say,
"A little angry today,"
"Joy filled, thank you,"
or
"Oh, so sad."
Each in its time.

But they want to know
about the outside.
They have to stop and listen;
they have to build trust
to talk about
way inside.
Sometimes
it causes them
to notice their inside, too.

Some people
only have time for
"Fine. . . .
Thanks for asking."

But sometimes
I need to get the
inside out.

Helping Hands

Pain had put me to bed
for many weeks,
my only entertainment
the birds that came
to my feeders.

I was grateful for them,
and I said a prayer of thanks
for their presence in my world,
their beauty,
and their songs.

As I lay in meditation one morning,
a mother cardinal
brought her baby to eat
from a jar of jelly,
hanging in the eaves.

She attended to him
and urged him,
feeding him with her beak
until he had learned
the technique.

I was amazed and wondered
how she knew
that jelly was something
her baby could eat.
It wasn't a part of nature,
but an invention of a human friend.

At that moment,
there was a mystical shift
in my consciousness.
Lord Christ appeared
and gently lifted the cardinal
to the feeder in His hands.

I thought,
How do any of us know
what we know intuitively?
Information is given to us
as we need it
if we stay connected to our Source.

Share the Walk

Tracks —
that's all we leave
in the sands of life.

The tide goes in.
The tide goes out.

Come walk with me.
Share the walk.
Share the now.

Hope

Sometimes
I feel nomadic.
A desert life is mine . . .
    parched,
        dry,
            searching,
                wandering.

Clinging to the hope
of a once-found oasis,
I move
    from barren day
        to chilling night.

Reaching toward a mirage
from time to time
diverts my attention.

But hope is all —
and enough for me.
Life is a mirage.
Hope is real.

Lifeline

I think of God
as a part of me
and me as a part of God.
He quietly dwells
within my soul
'til I desire to be whole
and give an assenting nod.

Can I be only part of myself?
Live only part of my life;
taste only part of the joy of living;
suffer just part of the strife;
know only part of the strength within;
love only part of my love;
give only part of what I have to give . . .
because I deny Him
the right to live
as my life?

How much I would miss!
How much I would waste!
How much I would never know!
I want to feel
all there is to feel,
to grow
all I am able to grow.

So I'll pray each day
He can use my life
in some way,
though it may be small.
I will open my heart,
where He can live
as I answer
His beckoning call.

Loneliness

Loneliness
turns me inward,
desolate and suffering,
utterly alone.
Despair wraps itself
tightly round me.
It will not let me go.

Tears of submission flow,
the hot rush of tears
held back so long
in the struggle
against withdrawal.
They flow timelessly,
endlessly.

My brain becomes hot
with the constant rush of thoughts.
Never time to sort them out;
only time to feel the sting,
the painfulness
of truths discovered
deep inside me.

Unknown feelings, hurts, emotions,
unexpressed before,
are born and recognized
as mine.
I am there
and I see me.

And I see God,
stepping from the shadows
of un-recognition
into the light
of a new beginning.
Loneliness
turns me outward.

Thief

I am a thief!
I stole from those
I love the most
their treasure,
their most precious possession—
their ability to relate in truth
to one another.

Wife and mother,
moderator,
peacemaker,
protector,
manipulator—
destructive force was I.

It took so long
for me to learn
that love can only happen
through encounter,
one authentic person
with the other.

Unrecoverable wealth,
priceless moments of truth
and opportunity,
are lost forever.
May true love
now put right
that which I did not mean
to plunder.

Demons

Unease and Worry,
demons of the mind.
We easily claim them
as a threat to our affairs.

They stir up the order
of our lives.
Bring doubts
and questions.

Why hasn't this worked?
Should I quit?
What is this telling me?

Let them go.
Give them space to pass.
They will only make trouble
if they can.

You are untouchable.
You are Spirit.
You are cherished —
a child of God.

Light of God

God heals.
I know that seems
like common faith
to most people;
but I learned the truth
firsthand.

I was in a deep depression,
concerned about my
failure to prevent
pain in my family.
I blamed myself and planned
to end my life for the good of all.

I could not contemplate this
under lesser circumstances.
I prayed and prayed,
and feeling a startling sense of peace,
I prepared to take the pills.
But first a minute to rest my weary heart.

As I lay on the bed,
the darkness of the day
reflected my intended actions.
Suddenly a great light
streamed in the window.
My body began to vibrate vigorously.
A feeling of intense love swept over me.

I felt loved as never before.
There was a warm glow in my heart.
The light continued to grow and surround me.
The vibrating energy I felt was pure bliss.
I knew I was loved.
I knew I was forgiven for any lack I felt.

I knew God wanted me to live
and use this knowledge
for the good of my family and others.
My life was changed forever.

Later, as I walked outside,
I could see this energy glowing in everything.
God is in all that He created.

It's Good

It's good
to be alive!
And
it's good to *know*
it's good
to be alive!

It's not easy
living,
really living.
Feeling,
being,
risking,
giving.
But
it's the knowing
that makes it good
to be alive!

Companions

Joy is!
Find it.
But do not be surprised
if it has a companion.

Sorrow and joy
often go hand in hand.
They may need each other.
They may live together.

But my prayer is
that my joy
may not produce
another's sorrow.

Church

Church —
not a building
but a heartfelt home
where boundaries fall.
Unity under God.
We're all God's children.

A global family
connected by
Love,
Spirit.

Designed to stick together
in united purpose,
service
the goal.

It is not I
but the Father within
Who does the work.
Divine work,
divine order.

Where two or three
are gathered in My name,
I am there
among them.

An Unseemly Cradle

Vapor swirls rise
on crisp damp air,
breath from warm nostrils.

The soft sound of doves
nesting for the night.

Pungent odors,
rhythmic sounds
from chewing creatures.

An earthy place,
a meager chamber
for the birth
announced by angel hosts.

The moan of birthing.
A baby's cry.
The darkness, now aglow,
brings forth the King.

Each year
the Child is born
yet again
in the unexpected earthiness
of our lives.

Shepherd

Jesus Christ —
instrument of God.
Messenger
between God
and his creation.

His ministry —
encounter
each one's need.

His church —
life
where he was,
when he was.

His message —
tend my sheep.

Divine Discontent

When my life becomes
less than fulfilling
and lacking direction,
where do I go for guidance?

Trusting in Spirit
to guide me,
I listen to my heart
for nudges and inner urges.

Open to Spirit's counsel
and stirred by personal desire,
I may step outside
my usual comfort zone.

My willingness
moves me forward,
taking small steps
at first.

As clarity becomes
more apparent,
I let go of reservations
and plunge ahead.

Fulfillment comes from
tackling a new "assignment"
and finding a place to give
myself.

Feelings

Feelings are tyrants,
changing our moods
on demand.

They can capture
a whole day,
if given free rein.

They are not as powerful
as they appear
at first awareness.

They can be counseled
by reason,
by thoughtful inspection.

They can be replaced
with understanding
and forgiveness.

We are empowered
to exercise
choice.

When Friends Leave

When friends leave
to serve
or satisfy a special personal need,
it leaves a hole
in my heart
that I can only fill
by remembering
the life we shared.

That's why I treasure
every moment of a friendship.
That's why I take the time
to really know my friends.
Then my heart
is so filled with memories,
I am overflowing with
gratitude and pleasure.

I can send them off
into their future
with a wish
for their greatest good
and a hope
that our lives will meet
at some time
in the awesome future.

Community

The purpose of Community
    is a sharing of
        the Body of Christ.

We each have
    our own little part
        of the beauty.

We each have
    our own unique
        Gifts of the Spirit.

Each of our gifts
    are given to us
        for the common good.

We are Community.
    We are all one body,
        made up of many gifts.

The gifts that are given to you
    are not only for your own self,
        but to build up the Community.

You don't have
    the full responsibility
        to put it all together.

Just discover
> your own gift
>> and use it for the good of all.

Our connectedness,
> the giving of our gifts,
>> is our holiness.

Birdhouse in Your Soul

My friend Donna gave me a painting
that she bought at an art fair.

Its title is
"Birdhouse in Your Soul."

She said,
"I knew this was for you."

I said,
"Oh ! Yes it is!"

Isn't it strange
that the artist painted me
and we've never met?

This was a God moment.
All the pieces came together.

A miracle
is like that.

Grace

Grace is such a thing
that sometimes
we don't notice it.
Or we call it
by another name.

Sometimes,
we call it bad luck
because it is not
the way we planned it.
Spirit planned it.

It takes time
to discern
the true intent
of a spiritual situation.
It takes contemplation.

We may have to
suffer through
in the darkness,
alone
for a time.

It takes openness
to the mystery
of spiritual lessons.
It takes faith
and trust in God.

Reassurance

When I am feeling
timid and unsure,
I come to You.

I have a deep conviction
that there is a Hand to hold.
I am not walking alone.

You are my Mother;
You are my Father;
God, my Creator.

You will lead me
on the chosen path,
the path of my destiny.

I will hold on tightly;
I will follow.
You may lead me.

Search for Myself

Where is my Self?
That part of me
that really is
Myself.

That part of me
that does not
work and strive
to Be.

That part
that need not
plan
but Is.

I need not search
outside my walls.
Just open up my heart
and let Me in.

Insecurity

God . . .

Why can't I be smart?
Rich in facts
and knowledge?

Why is my memory
such a storehouse
of butterflies,
gone so soon?

All I know
is what I feel,
what I experience.

Nobody cares
about that!

Good Enough

Good Enough is self-acceptance.
It's easy
to doubt.
It's easy
to find fault with yourself,
to lose faith.
But *Good Enough*
provides a spiritual haven
where peace of mind
begins to grow
and be nurtured
by the God within.
Good Enough
will never forsake you
once she has touched you.
She lives within you
because she is really
who you are.
She calls you by name.
She is your spiritual self.

Personality Trait

One of my
personality traits
tries to dominate.

Her name is
Perfectionism.
She troubles me.

When I make mistakes,
she tries to tell me
I'm not lovable.

I know we all have traits
that try to limit
our freedom to be.

As I've gotten older,
I have learned
to recognize her.

I can understand
that she was bred into me
long ago.

Then I have choices.
I can decide
what is *good enough*.

I don't have to be
driven by her.
I can relax a little.

I can do my best.
I can work with good intent
and spiritual guidance.

I can know
that I am a child of God
and I am always loved.

Unfinished

The Soul, like clay,
is fashioned
by the hands of many.
Never dry, ever changing,
forever becoming.
Retaining bits
of each hand
that has reached out
 to touch our life.

Left alone,
its growth would stop;
its shape unchanging
would harden as it is
and, ready for the kiln,
would cease to know
its striving
toward completion.

Surrender to Time

Time,
move through me.
Let me stand silently
that your blade
may pass cleanly.
Each scar is a victory,
a healing,
a growing,
an unexpected
opportunity for change.
Cut deeply,
oh blade of time.
I will not struggle
to resist the pain.
Scar tissue strengthens.
Time,
be my surgeon.

Growing Pains

Pain helps me grow.
Without it,
I would never know
the hidden resources
deep within me —
that inner strength
necessity brings forth,
the Self,
which deep emotion
brings to recognition,
and a sensitivity
to others' needs.
An appreciation
for the small,
significant,
beautiful
things in life.
A true sense of values.
My part
in His Plan.

Weather Maker

It's raining today outside.
But in my heart
is warm sunshine.
I am a weather maker.
Weather is a state of mind.

How Do We Hear?

At how many decibels
do we hear the cry
of another's soul?
The confused cry
of a disturbed child,
a teenager's staccato,
the feeble cry
    of the aged,
        the lonely?
The call of each one's need.

And how do we hear the joy?
The burst of life
in a newborn babe,
the eagerness
of the young child,
gulping life
with the appetite
of a young bird.
The joy of maturing
    and growing
        and loving.

How do we hear
the sounds of those
partaking in
the communion of life?
The multi-dimensional
experience of Being
and the discovery
that pain
    and joy
        have fused.

On Becoming Independent

Your fuzzy grey-brown shell
moves slightly
with the life enclosed inside.
I watch your struggling,
the lonely task
of life itself,
of becoming.
And then
the sharing of your beauty
with the waiting world,
with those who need
the flutter of a butterfly's wings
to catch their eyes
and help them see
the world around them,
as they follow your flight
down unknown,
untried paths.

I long to reach out,
to make it easier.
To open that shell
that surrounds you.
To free you,
to let you know
you are not alone.
But I can only watch.
I dare not touch too much.

My loving touch might just destroy
the time God planned
to make you strong,
to bring your folded, crumpled wings
the strength they need
to stretch,
to fly.

I hope you see my watching eyes
and feel my love,
my deep concern,
dear butterfly
in your grey-brown cocoon.

Being Present

lazy day
early summer
I sit on a grassy knoll

water sparkles
canoe floats slowly by
dip dip

mother pushes stroller
baby sleeping

joggers
puff puff

lovers walk hand in hand

young man fishes from the shore

elderly man
walks slowly up the path
tap tap
sounds his cane

he pauses
at the water's edge
lays his cane beside him
in the grass

slowly he steps
into the water
one step
two

and disappears

silence

his hat floats downstream

going Home

Will and Awareness

The brain can invent
both lightness and darkness—
great beauty
and great destruction,
calm or chaos.

Are you master
of your thoughts?
Where do you invest
your brain power?
Do you serve Spirit?

We spend much time
on earthly matters.
So much
seems critically important
but is not.

Passion and emotion
often storm through
the brain,
upsetting and shattering it,
creating unease.

We want things to happen
immediately!
But God never hurries.
He gives us all the time in eternity
to work and be joyful.

The spirit of calm is available
when we live today
with intention
and spiritual counsel
from the God within.

By an effort of will
and the awareness of Spirit,
life can be joyous,
and we can still the storms
of daily living.

Peace

We long for peace.
We think of peace as
being goodwill
toward each other.

Goodwill among
the nations,
the laying down
of arms.

But peace is
more than this.
It can only be understood
and realized in the heart.

It lies beneath
all the turmoil,
noise, and clamor
of the world.

It lies beneath
thought and feeling.
It is found in the deep, deep
silence and stillness of the soul.

It is Spirit.
It is God.
Seek daily for that still center,
the abiding place of Spirit.

Diversity

Segregation
must break the heart of God.
We all live in the same home.

But we often feel
discomfort with diversity.
We don't know how to be natural.

We don't know
what to say or how to hear.
Unfamiliar customs confuse us.

We should try diversity,
be deliberate about it.
We may hear with new ears.

We may find
new friendships
that stretch and challenge us.

They may challenge
our rigid ways of
being, doing, and knowing.

Reconciliation is essential
to the balance and wholeness
of God's Kingdom.

We need to see
our neighbors as ourselves.

Courage

Like Moses before the bush,
there is a fear
of being asked
to do the impossible.

What would God
ask of me
if I could listen
deeply enough?

God has BIG ideas!

What kind
of courage
could I find within
to answer yes?

What kind
of courage
would I need
to complete the task?

Yet I say
in prayer,
Thy Will, not mine,
be done.

Walking Around Blind

Sometimes I think
I see only a fraction
of what God has given me
in the grace of each day.

There are days
when I make myself
so busy with the *small stuff*
that I miss God's fabulous blessings.

We can become so accustomed
to the familiar
that it loses its significance,
 its power to bring joy, beauty, and healing.

When I take time to sit with God,
when I make space
for contemplation,
my focus becomes richer and fuller.

I see all that was created for me.
I wonder how I could miss
what is before my eyes,
the available treasures I did not see.

Under God's counsel,
I feel the abundance of His love.
I commit to letting go of
walking around blind
to His Presence in everything.

Striving

April is striving
to become spring,
hampered by
cold winds and rainy days.

She strives on
with sunny skies
to keep the order
that all nature expects.

Small sprouts of green
endure the cold.
Creatures come out
to seek nourishment.

Buds, tightly bound
through winter's cold,
burst forth
in expectation of fulfillment.

Divine order
takes precedence.
Striving is the law
of life.

Who are you?
Why are you here?
Reach for your purpose.
Strive on.

Find your gifts
and give them away.
The world is waiting.
Strive on.

Striving is the law of life.

Reverence for Life

God created a community
when He created physical life.
That community
is a part of Himself.
We are all one
in our Creator.

All of the solar kingdom,
mineral kingdom,
plant kingdom,
animal kingdom,
and human kingdom
make up this community.

We are all here together
to support life
in the larger community.
Each kingdom has a unique part to play,
with the common purpose
to serve Creator's Plan.

God gave humans
a special assignment.
He gave us dominion
over the other kingdoms.
To have dominion means
to be a steward.

We must be aware
of natural laws
and rhythms
and take responsibility
to care for and respect all life forms.
We are here to live in harmony.

And God said, "It is good."

Imagine

Spirit brooded,
alone and restless,
nothing to do.
Thinking, thinking.

Wouldn't it be nice
if I had something
to do?
Something besides brooding?

Suddenly it got brighter.
There was a brilliant light
in the space
and ground to walk on.

Wouldn't it be nice
if I had something to look at?
Some beauty to enjoy,
mountains to walk in?

Wouldn't it be nice
if there were waters
to swim in?
Sea creatures to watch?

Wouldn't it be nice
if the ground
was covered with plants and trees?
With flowers?

Wouldn't it be nice
if there were some animals
to walk with,
to play with?

And . . .
wouldn't it be nice
if there were other
beings to talk to?

Suddenly,
God had a good idea!
I'll create it!
And so He did.

Freedom

As we travel through life,
we may encounter
moments of disappointment
and unfulfilled expectations.

Daily life with
Friends, family, and community
is not always
a smooth highway.

Irritations and hurt feelings
often leave us with
a heavy burden
to carry.

The road
of resentment,
is a long,
lonely walk.

Emotional baggage
is heavy.
We try to get rid of it.
We give it to others to carry.

We must be willing to carry
our part of the load.
Working together
will lighten the burden.

Humility and love
and commitment to truth
open the blocked
intersections.

Freedom
from these times of stress
can only happen through
forgiveness and understanding.

Presence

Some say
there's a Presence
in their lives
that brings the random pieces together
in times of stress.

Unexplained by chance,
intuition suggests
it is planned
by a Holy Intelligence
that saw the need.

Astonishment and wonder
bring it to our attention.
Intuition informs us
that our faith
played a part.

When we make room for Spirit
to usher in new insights
and experiences,
we create the space
for unexpected blessings.

God is always ready
to do a new thing.
When it springs forth,
will we be ready
to receive?

Evolution of Consciousness

Sometimes things happen in our lives
that seem harsh,
    but we accommodate
        because we see no other way.
We don't see the good yet.
It's too far in the distance.

But time changes things.
It changes our perspective.

When we get the whole picture,
    we understand
        that good evolves over time.
We shouldn't be too quick to judge.

God . . .
    has all the time
        in the world.

Aging

Aging is a burden for some.
It's not an easy process.
In fact, it doesn't start
when you become elderly.
It starts when you are born
and continues on and on.

You notice it
when you are closer to death . . .
if there is such a thing.

Aging is about harvesting
the gems of learning
and dispensing with
the worn assumptions.

It requires courage,
honest discernment,
and a desire to lighten the load.

Aging is about
the freedom to embrace
the NOW . . . as it is.

It's about gratitude
for the gift of life
and faith in a timeless God.

Questions

At my age,
wouldn't you think
all the questions
would have found answers?

But still,
I travel uncharted territory.
I seek direction.

Even with God as my Guide,
it's a long journey
that never lacks surprises
and challenges.

I wonder . . .
Am I really asking
the right questions?

Perfect Love
For My Husband

Time has honed us,
taken off the sharp edges.
Life does that.
Love does that.

Age suits us.

We have our rhythms now.
Like waves in the ocean
we allow the tides
to take us in and out together.

The storms don't destroy us.
The winds are gentler.
We know we can make it
'til death do us part.

Powerlessness

When we feel powerless,
we want order in our lives.
The pain brings us down.

When we are humbled,
the search for meaning
makes us vulnerable and open.
Blessed are the poor in spirit.

Out of powerlessness,
God creates a new kind of power.
The last will be first,
and the first will be last.

This is often the time
when we see life anew
and we know . . .
ours is the kingdom of heaven.

God Cares

How does God
have time to notice
our wounds and suffering?
We plead for help.
We ask for mercy.
We claim our birthright
as sons and daughters.

God touched me
at a time such as this.
Severe pain and suffering
over an extended period
brought me to tears.
I was losing hope.
Discouragement
brought me to my knees.

As I reached out in prayer
with all my spirit,
God reached back,
and I felt a mystical hand
touching my head,
tenderly stroking my hair
like a father or mother.
Caring.
Comforting.

I know . . .
God cares.

Family Night

It's Sunday night,
Family night
at our house.

There's always
a discussion,
a lively discussion.

Everyone has something to say.
Everyone wants to be heard.
Everyone wants a turn.

Diversity is always
our standard approach —
a wide range of opinions,
just like the world.

But we can differ
and still show respect.
Nobody wants war;
nobody becomes abusive.
We can accept differences.

We can sit down
to dinner together,
enjoy the family,
and say "I love you"
when we take leave.

Love Is a Choice

What is love
but an open heartedness
that flows out.

You can't hoard real love.
You have to let it go
. . . freely.

Keeping your heart space open
is daily work.
It's your meditation.

It requires
a generous spirit,
willingness to serve,
and reluctance to judge.

It is a choice.

Living with Intention

One step we take,
one decision we choose,
something we do in a moment
leads to our future.

Our values should be
the guides that point the way
to the steps and choices we make,
leading us to our intended goals.

Living with intention
requires thought,
meditation,
and discernment.

We often forget
what really matters.
Then life becomes a puzzle
with pieces that don't fit.

Spiritual Guidance

Sleeping quietly one night,
I was roused by a need
to move and shift position.
I felt a sense of unease
in my whole body.

I turned over slowly
and found, to my surprise,
a man standing silently
beside my bed.
He appeared to be East Indian.

He wore a black robe
with a raised clerical collar
and a turbaned headpiece.
He simply looked at me,
saying nothing, observing.

He gave me no reason to fear,
but I cried out
and awoke my husband.
The man disappeared and
I haven't seen him again.

I believe he was there
to announce a change in my life,
a renewed focus on spirituality,
offering a personal invitation
to expand my spiritual growth.

A few months after his appearance
I enrolled in a seminary,
where I went on to grow
in spiritual understanding
and practices.

I wonder what the future holds?

I pray God will use my gifts.

Whose Energy Is It?

Do your work quietly,
like flowers
opening to sunlight.

Render service gently
as your gift to life.
Just do your best.

When tension arises,
don't let *your* energy storm through,
trying to be right.

What a waste of energy!
Whose is it anyway?
God's energy.

Turn your heart and hands to God
and work together.
It's all God's work.

Jesus and Me

I know theology.
I've even taught theology.
I have a Ph.D.
in Religious Studies.

But . . .
what I know about Jesus
I've learned from Him
in my heart.

A companion
on the journey of life,
He has always been there
for me.

We talk about the rocky road
and the fields of bliss.
We share our love
and our love of our Father.

Jesus is my brother,
my prayer partner.

Walking Contemplation: A Word Picture

I walked with God today.
A brisk step has He
to keep the cadence
of my morning stride,
even as my breath comes fast
and my heartbeat drums inside.

Released to play,
my black lab romps
through fields of grass.
She teases pheasants from their nests
and sniffs out trampled beds
where deer have slept and passed.

Four brown eyes,
round as saucers,
two pairs of ears
behind a log I see.
Rabbits bound in two directions.
They needn't be afraid of me.

Purple sweet peas,
wild yellow snapdragons,
bright red berries.
The greenish blue of grapes
not yet ripe.
The color of God's palette.

A gentle breeze
cools my dampening skin.
Dog runs through puddles.
I hear her pant.
The sun feels hot.

Under my feet
the path is hard.
I feel grounded.
Solid.
I know God Is.
God lives in all of this.

Songbirds chirp and fly
between the trees.
A blue dragonfly darts.
A dove calls,
I answer.
Morning salutation.

A shaded cove of trees.
Damp earth smell.
Dark brown fungus grows,
companion to a dead oak
that provides a
woodpecker residence.

A spring bubbles noisily.
I spy twinkling twin blue lakes
in the distance.
Cattails stand guard
around their shores.
Lily pads float lazily.

White egrets
stand one-footed
in the shallows.
Appetites satisfied.
Resting.
Watching.

False dandelion,
mullein, and ragweed brown
have taken retirement.
Goat's beard puffs
prepare
to take flight.

The orange of
Turk's cap lilies
catches my eye,
an unexpected surprise!
Solomon's seal
drips black berries.

I taste the saltiness of me.
It stings my eyes.
Cleansing,
healthy.
I ache a little.
It feels good.

Is this all commonplace
to you, my Lord?
I never get enough!
The beauty of creation
heals,
restores my calm.

On daily walks with You
my senses come alive.
Who am I
that You give all this
abundant grace
beyond my expectation?

Requiescat

When I die,
sing glad songs!
Tell a story of life everlasting.
Weep for your loneliness
but not for me.
I go with joy,
unafraid,
with arms outstretched,
eager for this new experience.
Don't look upon my lifeless shell.
It served my needs,
but I'll be gone.
Remember what you will.
No tended grave,
cold and lonely.
Blow me to the winds
in some sweet spot
I would have loved.
Free my body with my soul
and tend me in your heart.

About the Author

Sharon Freeman is a retired non-denominational minister. Her mother was a deeply committed Christian, who taught her to pray and meditate every day from an early age. She grew up attending a Methodist church and has belonged to several denominations over her lifetime. Currently, she's a member of a Unity spiritual center, which teaches the oneness of all people with God and the validity of many paths to the Divine.

Sharon first earned a B.A. in Psychology and Education from Macalester College in St. Paul, Minnesota, and began her career as a primary teacher. Later, at the University of Minnesota, she became certified to teach special education students and continued in that career for 25 years. Her special love was teaching students diagnosed with autism. Because of health issues, she took an early retirement from teaching at age 65.

After she "retired," Sharon was inspired to go back to school to learn more about spiritual practices and work as a spiritual counselor. She obtained certification through The Cenacle in Wayzata, Minnesota, and later traveled to Shalem Institute in Bethesda, Maryland, to study for a two-year certification as a spiritual director. A growing interest in religious theology prompted her to continue studies at St. Catherine University in St. Paul, Minnesota, where she obtained a Masters in Theology. Encouraged and inspired by the dean of Sancta Sophia Seminary in Tahlequah, Oklahoma, Sharon completed studies for ordination and earned a Ph.D. in Religious Studies at the age of 75. Although never the pastor of a church, she's performed all the usual Christian ceremonies for other ministers.

Family has always been the most important focus for Sharon. She and her husband Harold have been married 64 years. They enjoy travel and have accrued many travel memories, one of the most significant being their trip to the Holy Lands. They have three grown children, who are married, and one adult granddaughter. All live in the Minneapolis area, and the family enjoys a tradition of Sunday night dinners together.

Over the years, black labs have been a cherished part of the Freeman family. Besides dogs, Sharon loves birds. The bird feeders on her deck in the woods invite many visitors such as cardinals, sparrows, chickadees, and to her delight — hummingbirds. On one occasion, she found a baby owl on her back steps. Squirrels jump from roof to feeder providing additional entertainment. For Sharon, nature is a constant source of inspiration and joy and a gift from God.

At age 84, Sharon continues to write so she can share her inspirations and what she's learned over a lifetime of prayer, study, and worship.

www.ingramcontent.com/pod-product-compliance
Lightning Source LLC
Chambersburg PA
CBHW031414040426
42444CB00005B/556